A Special Gift
For

_____

From

_____

Date

_____

Faith

Edited by Paul C. Brownlow

Brownlow

Brownlow Publishing Company, Inc.

Little Treasures
Miniature Books

FROM FRIEND TO FRIEND

GOLDEN MOMENTS—
*Hope & Inspiration from
Leaves of Gold*

PRECIOUS PROMISES

TREASURES FROM THE PSALMS

DEAR TEACHER

QUILTED HEARTS—*When Friends Are Near Hearts Abound in Love*

MOTHER—*A Little Book of Inspiration*

FOR MY SECRET PAL

ANGELS OF FRIENDSHIP—*Gather Half Their Joy*

FAITH—*All Things Are Possible to Those Who Believe*

HOPE—*If Hope Were Not Heart Would Break*

LOVE—*Love and You Shall Be Loved*

Contents

CHAPTER ONE

The Adventure of Faith

We cannot tell what may happen
to us in the strange medley of life.
But we can decide what happens
in us—how we can take it,
what we do with it—and that

is what really counts in the end.
How to take the raw stuff of life
and make it a thing of worth and
beauty—that is the test of living.
Life is an adventure of faith,
if we are to be victors over it,
not victims of it.

Both faith and fear sail into the
harbor of your mind, but only faith
should be allowed to anchor.

Pin your faith on no man's sleeve;
have faith in God.

Faith plus hope is powerful.

There Is
No Unbelief

There is no unbelief;
Whoever plants a seed
beneath the sod
And waits to see it push
away the clod—
He trusts in God.

ELIZABETH YORK CASE

Give Me Faith

Lord, give me faith!—to live
from day to day,
With tranquil heart to do
my simple part,
And, with my hand in Thine,
just go Thy way.
Lord, give me faith!—to trust,
if not to know;
With quiet mind in all things.
Thee to find,

And, child-like to go where
Thou wouldst have me go.
Lord, give me faith!—
to leave it all to Thee,
The future is Thy gift,
I would not lift
The veil Thy love has hung
'twixt it and me.

JOHN OXENHAM

I pray that out of his glorious riches
he may strengthen you with power
through his Spirit in your
inner being, so that Christ may dwell
in your hearts through faith.

EPHESIANS 3:16

❧

It's faith in something and
enthusiasm for something that
makes life worth looking at.

OLIVER WENDELL HOLMES

$\mathcal{F}$aith lifts up shining arms
and points to a happier world where
our loved ones await us.

HELEN KELLER

$\mathcal{G}$od doesn't call us to be successful.
He calls us to be faithful.

$\mathcal{T}$here is no great future for any
people whose faith has burned out.

RUFUS M. JONES

What Is Faith?

Sight is not faith, and hearing is not faith, neither is feeling faith; but believing when we neither see, hear, nor feel is faith; and everywhere the Bible tells us our salvation is to be by faith. Therefore we must believe before we feel, and often against our feelings, if we would honor God by our faith.

HANNAH WHITALL SMITH

*F*eed your faith and your doubts
will starve to death.

*L*ove the Lord, all his saints!
The Lord preserves the faithful,
but the proud he pays back in full.

PSALM 31:23

*F*aith is the light of the
flame of love.

We never become truly spiritual
by sitting down and wishing
to become so. You must undertake
something so great that you cannot
accomplish it unaided.

PHILLIPS BROOKS

Faith and conviction become
stronger when attacked.

ANONYMOUS

A Good Haven

Our life is not a mere fact:
it is a movement, a tendency,
a steady, ceaseless progress
toward an unseen goal.
To desire and strive
to be of some service to the world,
to aim at doing something
which shall really increase

the happiness and welfare
and virtue of mankind—
this is a choice which is possible
for all of us: and surely it is
a good haven to sail for.

HENRY VAN DYKE

The smallest seed
of faith is better than
the largest
fruit of happiness.

HENRY DAVID THOREAU

Our greatest glory consists
not in never failing,
but in rising
every time we fall.

OLIVER GOLDSMITH

A perfect faith would lift us
absolutely above fear.

GEORGE MACDONALD

*A*ll work that is worth
anything is done in faith.

ALBERT SCHWEITZER

*F*aith in mankind will be a reality
when they stop hauling money
in armored cars.

Mustard Seed Faith

For if you have faith even as small

as a tiny mustard seed you could

say to this mountain, "Move!"

and it would go far away.

Nothing would be impossible.

MATTHEW 17:20

CHAPTER TWO

The Prize

Of all the prizes

That earth can give,

This is the best:

To find Thee, Lord,

A living Presence near

And in Thee rest!

Friends, fortune, fame,

Or what might come to me—

I count all loss

If I find not

Companionship

With Thee!

AUTHOR UNKNOWN

❦

CHAPTER THREE

❦

Faith Is...

Faith is to believe what
we do not see, and the reward
of this faith is to see
what we believe.

AUGUSTINE

*W*here love is there is faith.

ANONYMOUS

I Believe

I believe in the sun,
even if it does not shine.
I believe in love,
even if I do not feel it.
I believe in God,
even if I do not see him.

HANS KUNG

The principal part of faith
is patience.

GEORGE MACDONALD

Faith is courage; it is creative
while despair is always destructive.

D. S. MUZZEY

All things are possible to him
that believeth.

MARK 9:23

Faith is a grasping of
Almighty power; the hand of man
laid on the arm of God,
the grand and blessed hour
in which the things impossible
to me become the possible,
O Lord, through Thee.

A. E. HAMILTON

Nothing will ever be attempted
if all possible objections
must be first overcome.

SAMUEL JOHNSON

The only limit to our realization
of tomorrow will be our doubts
of today. Let us move forward
with strong and active faith.

FRANKLIN D. ROOSEVELT

God of our life,
through all the circling years,
We trust in Thee;
In all the past,
through all our hopes and fears,
Thy hand we see.
With each new day,
when morning lifts the veil,
We own Thy mercies,
Lord, which never fail.

HUGH THOMSON KERR

Faith is the force of life.

LEO TOLSTOY

He who is small in faith will never be great in anything but failure.

Without faith, we are as stained glass windows in the dark.

ANONYMOUS

*F*aith, in its very nature,
demands action.
Faith is action—
never a passive attitude.

PAUL E. LITTLE

*I*t is better to trust the Lord
than to put confidence in men.
It is better to take refuge in him
than in the mightiest king!

PSALM 118:8, 9

Kinship

Who reaps the grain
and plows the sod
Must feel a kinship
with his God:

For there's so much
on earth to see
That marks the
hand of Deity.

When blossom springs
from tiny shoot:

When orchard yields
its luscious fruit:

When sap is running
from great trees—
On all occasions
such as these

The man who breathes
fresh country air
Must know full well
that God is there.

ROGER WINSHIP STUART

Trust and Obey

Faith and obedience are
bound up in the same bundle;
he that obeys God trusts God;
and he that trusts God obeys God.
He that is without faith
is without works,
and he that is without works
is without faith.

CHARLES H. SPURGEON

*F*aith makes all things possible...
love makes all things easy.

D. L. MOODY

*G*uidance means that I
can count on God.
Commitment means that God
can count on me.

In the Sunshine

There in the Sunshine
are my highest aspirations...
I can look up and see
their beauty,
believe in them.
And try to follow
where they lead.

LOUISA MAY ALCOTT

*N*ow faith is being sure
of what we hope for and
certain of what we do not see.
This is what the ancients were
commended for. By faith
we understand that the universe
was formed at God's command,
so that what is seen was not made
out of what was visible.

HEBREWS 11:1-3

God's Witnesses

I need not shout my faith.
Thrice eloquent
Are quiet trees and
the green listening sod;

Hushed are the stars,
whose power is never spent;

The hills are mute:
yet how they speak of God!

CHARLES HANSON TOWNE

Faith does nothing alone—
nothing of itself,
but everything under God,
by God, through God.

WILLIAM STOUGHTON

The strengthening of faith comes
through staying with it
in the hour of trial.

CATHERINE MARSHALL

Real faith is not the stuff dreams are made of; rather it is tough, practical and altogether realistic. Faith sees the invisible but it does not see the nonexistent.

A. W. TOZER

Faith is not a sense, nor sight, nor reason, but taking God at His Word.

ARTHUR BENONI EVANS

❧

CHAPTER FOUR

❧

High Flight

Oh! I have slipped the surly
bonds of earth
And danced the skies on
laughter-silvered wings;
Sunward I've climbed, and joined
the tumbling mirth
Of sun-split clouds—and done
a hundred things

You have not dreamed of—
wheeled and soared and swung
High in the sunlit silence.
Hov'ring there,
I've chased the shouting wind
along, and flung
My eager craft through
footless halls of air.

Up, up the long, delirious,
burning blue

I've topped the wind-swept
heights with easy grace
Where never lark,
or even eagle flew—
And, while with silent lifting
mind I've trod
The high untrespassed
sanctity of space,
Put out my hand and
touched the face of God.

JOHN GILLESPIE MAGEE, JR.

CHAPTER FIVE

The Wings of Faith

To have faith is to have wings.

JAMES M. BARRIE

If doubt overtakes you,
stop for a faith lift.

ANONYMOUS

$\mathcal{L}$et love and faithfulness
never leave you; bind them around
your neck, write them on
the tablet of your heart.

PROVERBS 3:3

$\mathcal{I}$t's not hard to make decisions
when you know
what your values are.

ROY DISNEY

Drawing Nigh

Whoso draws nigh to God one step

through doubtings dim,

God will advance a mile

in blazing light to him.

AUTHOR UNKNOWN

Heaven's Glories

No coward soul is mine,

No trembler in the world's

storm-troubled sphere:

I see Heaven's glories shine,

And faith shines equal,

arming me from fear.

EMILY BRONTE

*H*ow would a person ever know
whether his faith was weak or strong
unless it has been tried and tested?

ANONYMOUS

*F*aith is a living, daring confidence
in God's grace, so sure and certain
that a man could stake his life
on it a thousand times.

MARTIN LUTHER

After all,
what do we ask of life,
here or indeed hereafter,
but to serve, to live,
to commune with our
fellowmen and with ourselves;
and from the lap of earth
to look up into the
face of God?

MICHAEL FAIRLESS

The steps of faith fall on the seeming void and find the rock beneath.

WALT WHITMAN

I have fought the good fight,
I have finished the course,
I have kept the faith.

2 TIMOTHY 4:7

Give to faith what belongs to faith.

ANONYMOUS

My Prayer

Oh, not for more or longer days,
dear Lord,
My prayer shall be—
But rather teach me
how to use the days
Now given me.

I ask not more of pleasure or of joy
For this brief while—
But rather let me
for the joys I have
Be glad and smile.

I ask not ownership
of vast estates
Nor piles of gold—
But make me generous
with the little store
My hands now hold.

Nor shall I ask that life should
give to me Another friend—
Just keep me true to those I have,
dear Lord,
Until the end.

B. Y. WILLIAMS

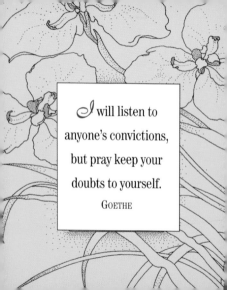

I will listen to anyone's convictions, but pray keep your doubts to yourself.

GOETHE

Pleasing God

You can never please God without
faith, without depending on him.
Anyone who wants to come to
God must believe there is a God
and that he rewards those who
sincerely look for him.

HEBREWS 11:6

When faith is lost,
when honor dies,
the man is dead.

J. G. WHITTIER

Understanding is the reward of faith.
Therefore seek not to understand that
thou mayest believe, but believe that
thou mayest understand.

AUGUSTINE

My Refuge

That man is perfect in faith
who can come to God in the utter
dearth of his feelings and desires,
without a glow or an aspiration,
with the weight of low thoughts,
failures, neglects, and wandering
forgetfulness, and say to Him,
"Thou art my refuge."

GEORGE MACDONALD

Faith is not a pill you take
but a muscle you use.

He that has lost faith,
what has he left to live on?

PUBLILIUS SYRUS

For he guards the course
of the just and protects
the way of his faithful ones.

PROVERBS 2:8

Beneath Thy Wings

Glory to Thee, my God,
this night

For all the blessings
of the light;

Keep me, O keep me,
King of kings,

Beneath Thine own
almighty wings.

THOMAS KEN

It is never a question
with any of us of faith or no faith;
the question always is,
"In what or in whom
do we put our faith?"

ANONYMOUS

The greatest act of faith takes place
when a man finally decides
that he is not God.

A ship in harbour is safe,
but that is not what
ships are built for.

WILLIAM SHEDD

*I*t is the art of mankind
to polish the world,
and everyone who works
is scrubbing in some part.

HENRY DAVID THOREAU

*T*hough you have not
seen him, you love him;
and even though you do
not see him now, you believe
in him and are filled with an
inexpressible and glorious joy,
for you are receiving
the goal of your faith,
the salvation of your souls.

1 Peter 1:8, 9

*A*ll I have seen teaches me to trust
the creator for all I have not seen.

RALPH WALDO EMERSON

*F*aith is simply the welcome
of the one who says "Here I am."
And taking that as our starting point,
we can be on our way.

JACQUES ELLUL

My Faith

My faith looks up to Thee,

Thou Lamb of Calvary,

Savior divine:

Now hear me while I pray;

Take all my guilt away,

O let me from this day

Be wholly Thine.

RAY PALMER

$\mathcal{L}$et us have faith that
right makes might,
and in that faith let us
to the end dare to do our
duty as we understand it.

ABRAHAM LINCOLN

❧

CHAPTER SIX

❧

God in the Morning

I met God in the morning
When my day was at its best,
And His presence came like sunrise,
Like a glory in my breast.

All day long the Presence lingered,
All day long He stayed with me,
And we sailed in perfect calmness
O'er a very troubled sea.

Other ships were blown
and battered,
Other ships were sore distressed,
But the winds that seemed
to drive them
Brought to us a peace and rest.

Then I thought of other mornings,
With a keen remorse of mind,
When I too had loosed the moorings,
With the Presence left behind.

So I think I know the secret,
Learned from many
a troubled way:

You must seek Him
in the morning
If you want Him
through the day!

RALPH SPAULDING CUSHMAN

CHAPTER SEVEN

Faith of Our Fathers

Faith builds a bridge from
this world to the next.

Faith is: dead to doubts, dumb to
discouragements, blind to
impossibilities.

ANONYMOUS

There are a thousand ways
of pleasing God, but not one
without faith.

Faith hears the inaudible,
sees the invisible,
believes the incredible,
and receives the impossible.

A perfect faith
lifts us above fear.

Thou Dost Not Fall

It fortifies my soul to know
That, though I perish, truth is so:
That, howsoe'er I stray and range,
Whate'er I do, Thou dost not change.
I steadier step when I recall
That, if I slip, Thou dost not fall.

ARTHUR HUGH CLOUGH

A simple, childlike faith in a Divine
Friend solves all the problems that
come to us by land or sea.

HELEN KELLER

*T*o believe with certainty,
we must begin by doubting.

ANONYMOUS

*F*aith sees by the ears.

ANONYMOUS

*S*trong faith can only be produced
amid darkness, discouragement,
and seemingly hopeless situations.
Strong muscles are produced
in the gymnasium of necessity.

A. P. GOUTHEY

*F*aith has no merit where human
reason supplies the proof.

ST. GREGORY

*Y*ou can do
very little with faith,
but you can do nothing
without it.

SAMUEL BUTLER

*B*e on your guard:
stand firm in the faith;
be men of courage;
be strong.

1 CORINTHIANS 16:13, 14

A Woman's Faith

Historically, most of the great bursts
of brilliance have originated
with men, but over and over
we can see that the continuity
and idealism of women have
accounted for the improvement
of the lot of mankind. I have
always felt it is a privilege to be

a woman. We give the durability,
the determined patience to keep our
eyes set on the star of peace for
mankind. In our hearts, we have
the faith to know that one day
we shall find it.

LADY BIRD JOHNSON

Faith of Our Fathers

Faith of our fathers! living still
In spite of dungeon, fire and sword;
O how our hearts beat high with joy
Whene'er we hear that glorious word!
Faith of our fathers, holy faith,
We will be true to thee till death.

FREDERICK W. FABER

Faith is always
at a disadvantage; it is
a perpetually defeated
thing which survives
all its conquerors.

G. K. CHESTERTON

He who
prays for rain
should always
carry an umbrella.

*F*aith will beget in us three things:
Vision, Venture, Victory.

GEORGE W. RIDOUT

*F*or the Lord loves the just and will
not forsake his faithful ones. They
will be protected forever.

PSALM 37:28

God Never Changeth

Let nothing disturb thee,
Nothing affright thee;
All things are passing;
God never changeth;
Patient endurance
Attaineth to all things;
Who God possesseth
In nothing is wanting;
Alone God sufficeth.

HENRY WADSWORTH LONGFELLOW

$\mathcal{F}$aith is the daring of the soul to go
farther than it can see.

WILLIAM NEWTON CLARKE

$\mathcal{D}$oubt is the vestibule which all
must pass before they can enter
the temple of wisdom.

COLTON

*F*or this reason, ever since I heard
about your faith in the Lord Jesus
and your love for all the saints,
I have not stopped giving thanks
for you, remembering you
in my prayers.

EPHESIANS 1:15, 16

*K*nowledge of things
divine escapes us through
want of faith.

GREEK PROVERB

*G*ods fade; but God abides
and in man's heart
Speaks with the clear
unconquerable cry
Of energies and hopes
that can not die.

JOHN ADDINGTON SYMONDS

*F*aith draws the poison from every
grief, takes the sting from every loss
and quenches the fire of every pain.

One who fears limits his activities.
Failure is only the opportunity to more
intelligently begin again.

HENRY FORD

The world is round and the place
which may seem like the end may
also be only the beginning.

IVY BAKER PRIEST

Spend your time in nothing which you know must be repented of; in nothing on which you might not pray the blessing of God; in nothing which you could not review with a quiet conscience on your dying bed; in nothing which you might not safely and properly be found doing if death should surprise you in the act.

RICHARD BAXTER

A people without
faith in God
and themselves
cannot survive.

*F*aith is trust.
By faith I mean a trust
in God's unknown,
unfelt, untried goodness
and mercy.

MARTIN LUTHER